When God Smiled At Me

RAINBOW GAZING

By
Angel Bryan Z. Ocampo

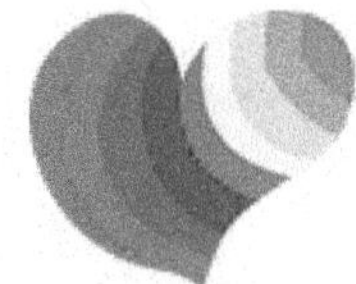

CONTENTS

PREFACE

The verses and real-life stories inscribed in this book contain a meaningful journey as intensely and ably compiled by the Author. No one, perhaps, could describe—with complete sincerity and commitment—the hardships and difficulties, including achievements and deep happiness than those who experienced it. They could say, God has answered their prayers as if they found gold at the end of a rainbow.

This is the reason why "When God Smiled At Me: RAINBOW GAZING" is being written to become a published book to touch and convey to readers its meaningful glances and lessons as its real life stories depict love, pain, hardships, as well as positivity, acceptance, and achievements, making this book a masterpiece.

ANGEL BRYAN Z. OCAMPO is undoubtedly among those great writers of today that have adeptly penned their writings through real thoughts and emotions, facts and experiences.

NOAH'S SMILE

DESSERTS FOR STRESSED

BLESSED TO BE STRESSED

Busyness is keeping us away to appreciate small things. Little did we know these are as beautiful and essential as big things.

Desserts for stressed...

Don't Overthink

Thinking too much makes our life more complicated. Things become heavy because we let our minds think heavily. Free our minds from worrying too much. This quarantine, God will provide.

> *Angels can fly (so high) because they take themselves lightly.*
> \- G.K. Chesterton

Noah's smile

Desserts for stressed...

Smell the Flowers

Take some time to pause and smell the flowers. Look around you how relaxing the ambiance is! The world offers us beautiful views to appreciate and enjoy God's magnificent creations.

Like a flower, keep blooming but stay rooted

Noah's smile

Desserts for stressed...

Do Gardening

Quarantanim is one of the productive things to do this pandemic. PlanTitas/Titos are now enjoying their lives taking care of plants. Because of your love for gardening, you can have your food on the table

Craving for Veggie Salad? Yummy!

Noah's smile

Desserts for stressed...

Sing your fave Songs

Due to your busy schedule, you don't have the time to sing your favorite song.
With CoVID-EOKE, you have now your ample time to sing the songs of your life (at home). Sing as if no one is listening. Out of tune (never mind)

I did it my way…way…way ..heyyyyyyyy!

Noah's smile

Desserts for stressed...

Have Moviemarathon

No time to watch movies outside because you're tired from work. With the present situation, the more you can't watch in movietheaters. However, lockdown yourself and watch the movies you have shelves at home. Enjoy watching with your family.

Don't forget the popcorns!

Noah's smile

Desserts for stressed...

Schedule a Danxercise

No gym due to CoVid? Never been a problem. Zumba and exercise video lessons can now be accessed easily. Apps can also be downloaded to take Exercise 101. One can also have Do It Yourself Danxercise at home. As they say, 'Dance as if no one is watching.'

My heart goes shalala-la-la-

Noah's smile

Desserts for stressed...

Learn Cooking 101

Time to experiment! Enough time is given to explore the kitchen. Your family may always feel hungry this lockdown. Cook from scratch. Cook with love. QuaSina is waiting to be explored to serve delicious food.

To paraphrase, the way to someone's heart is through someone's stomach.

Noah's smile

Desserts for stressed...

Explore the House

When did you really visit the corners of your house? Have you checked the appliances? Your house misses your magic touch. It is waiting for your personal care. Now, more than ever, is the right time to do some general cleaning and fixing. Use this time to make your house COOL (C-lean, O-rderly, O-rganize & L-ively).

Indeed, there's no place like home

Noah's smile

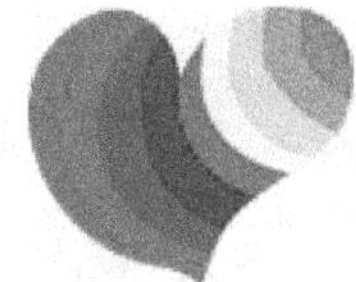

Desserts for stressed...

Rest and Sleep

Work, no matter how we love it, gives stress if we are overworked. We even make our home the extension of our work that really exhausts our body and mind. We forget that we are humans, too. All humans need some rest and sleep. Don't feel guilty even God rested on the seventh day.

Quiet
pls...zzzzZzzzzZzzZzzzZZZZZZzzZZzzZ

Noah's smile

Desserts for stressed...

Smile & Laugh often

Laughter is still the best antidote. Proverbs 17:22 (NIV) A cheerful heart is good medicine, but a crushed spirit dries up the bones. Many studies have shown that smiling and laughing will make you young and keep you healthy. Greet others with a smile. Laugh with your mistakes. Laugh often with happy memories. Be happy. Choose to be happy. Stay happy.

LOL ...HaHahahahahahaahahaahahaah

Noah's smile

Spend FaMEaLy Time

When was the last time you eat together as one family? Eating together is a form of family bonding time.The love of a family is the best stress-buster. It makes you whole and complete. Make the most of the lockdown period. So, always spend quality time with your family.

Happy Eating!

Noah's smile

Desserts for stressed...

Say NO

Most of our stress comes from pleasing people.We always say yes to get their approval. Saying No is not being a self-centered person. It is just taking care of our personal self. Making more time to relax to become more productive and effective.

Not now, maybe next time.

Noah's smile

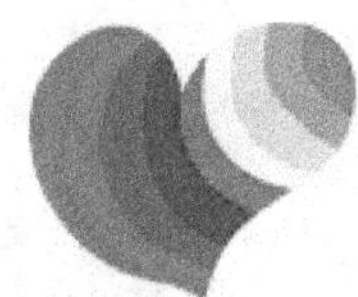

Desserts for stressed...

Avoid Toxic People

Life is too short to spend our lives with wrong people. There are really people who are not happy with their lives that they like to destroy good people. Keeping yourself away from them is one way to make your life peaceful. Never argue with them because they only listen to things they want to hear. Walk away from them when the respect is no longer served.

No time for you. Bye!

Noah's smile

Desserts for stressed...

Sweet Treats

Anyone who has a sweet tooth can't resist desserts such as the silky smooth leche flan, nutritious and colorful fruit salad, or refreshing halo-halo. These are desserts for stressed. Take a good amount of them to destress and unwind. Life is sweet and beautiful to be stressed.

Stay Calm. Stay Sweet.

Noah's smile

Desserts for stressed...

Pray

Whether you're okay or not okay, always the best thing to do is pray.

If you're happy, pray. If you're sad, pray. Sunny day or rainy day, pray.

Prayer is our communication with God. He hears even our most silent cries. Lift everything to Him – our worries, our concerns, & our stress.

Pray without ceasing.

1 Thessalonians 5: 17 ESV

Noah's smile

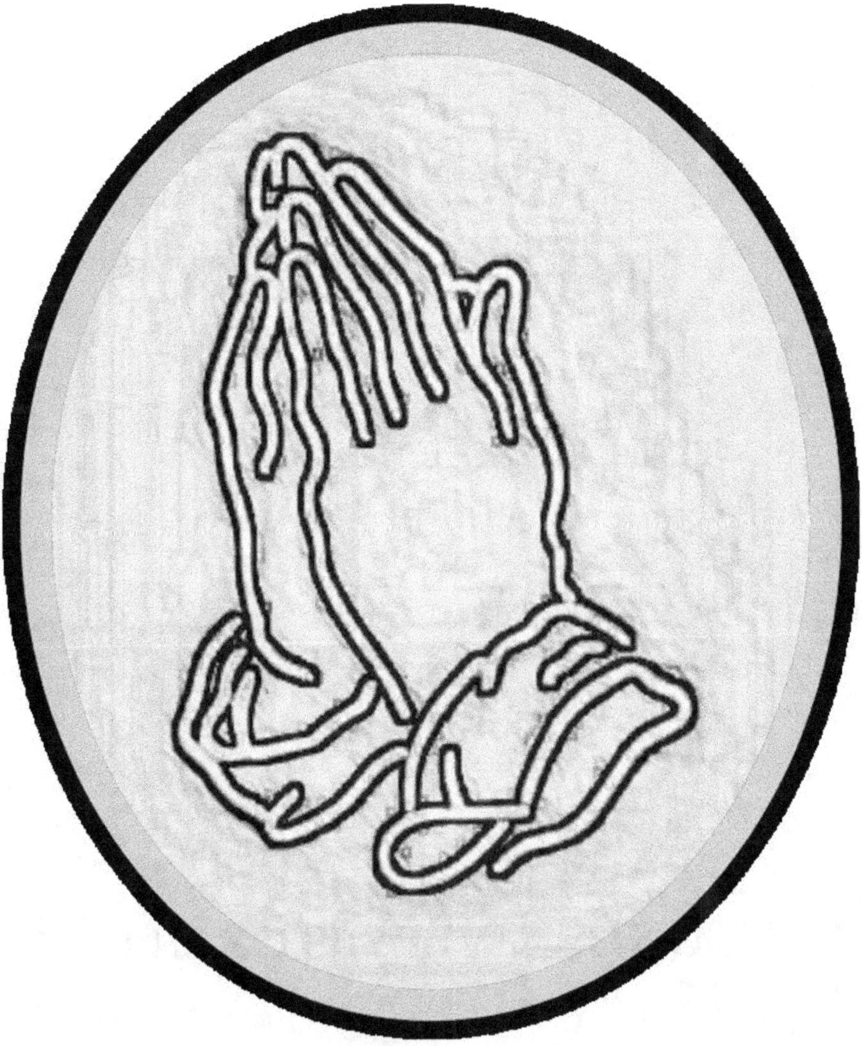

Disclaimer: Image not mine / cttro

Never underestimate the power of prayers.
Prayers can move mountains and can change life.

RAINBOW HUES

SONGS & VERSES OF LIFE

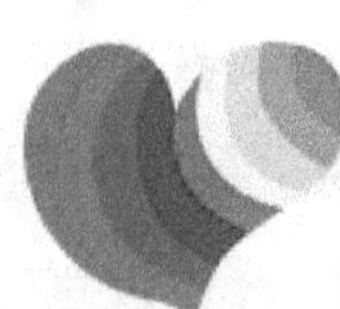

Show YOUR COLORful Tones

Our choices in life somehow define who we are and what we are passionate about. Even with the songs we sing become the music of our soul and verses we follow become our guiding light in life.

Songs of life...

Ikaw na ang Bahala

These trying times have made our lives difficult. This pandemic has brought sudden changes in our way of living. Different sectors have been largely affected – education, health, livelihood and business. With all of these, we sing to You, Lord, Ikaw na ang Bahala sa Amin Ama. We are praying for better days ahead.

Rainbow Hues

Verses of life...

Psalm 56:3 TPT

CoVid-19 has brought us fears and tears. Some died. Others lost their job. Many are helpless. Lord, all of our concers and worries, we all surrender to You. As we pray, "But in the day that I'm afraid. I lay all my fears before You and trust in You with all my heart."

Rainbow Hues

Songs of life...

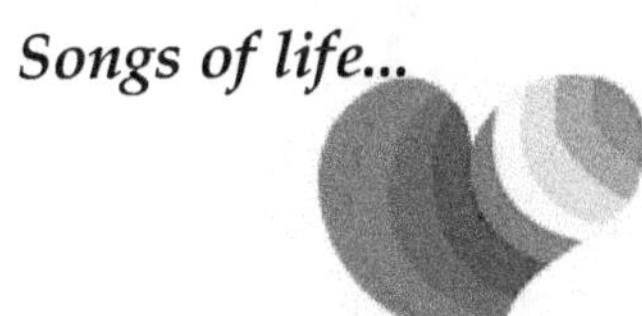

Above All

No possession, no power, no position can ever match Your glory. No philosophy, no intellect, no giant minds can ever compare to Your wisdom. No kingdom, thrones can ever replace Your manger. No disease, no sickness even CoVid that You can't heal. And we all sing, Above all.

Rainbow Hues

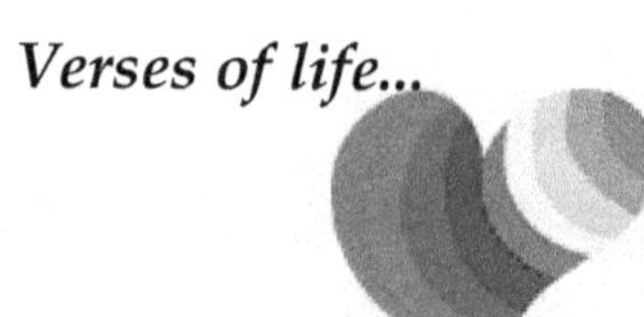

Luke 1:37 KJB

God created the universe. He created you and me. What else can He not possibly do? To defeat this virus seems impossible to men. But with God, we will win this battle against CoVid-19. As we pray, "For with God nothing shall be impossible."

Rainbow Hues

Songs of life...

I Offer My life

The life we are enjoying is not ours. God has only entrusted this to make the world a better place. The talents, the skills, the mind, the heart, we all borrowed them from God. What we do with our lives is what we offer to God. This pandemic what are you willing to offer? And we all sing, Lord, I offer, to You, my life.

Rainbow Hues

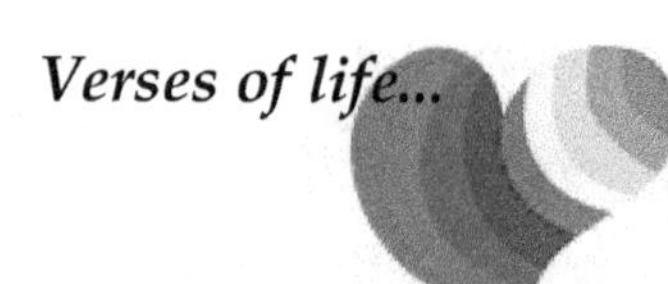

Psalm 139:14 NIV

Take good care of yourself this pandemic. Follow health protocols. Don't be too hard to yourself, precious child of God. We are God's masterpiece – well-formed and created. As we pray, "I praise You because I am fearfully and wonderfully made; your works are wonderful, I know that full well."

Rainbow Hues

Songs of life...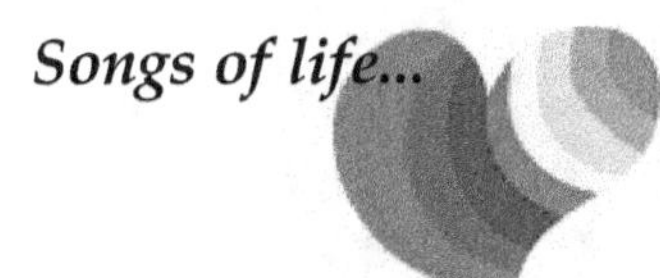

I See You Lord

Do you see God and feel His presence these difficult times? We call God whenever problems come. When these problems go, we tend to forget Him. Our eyes can not see how He works in our lives. With deep and strong faith in Him, each day He is watching us. Seeing Him is by believing. And we all sing, I see You, Lord whenever I pray.

Rainbow Hues

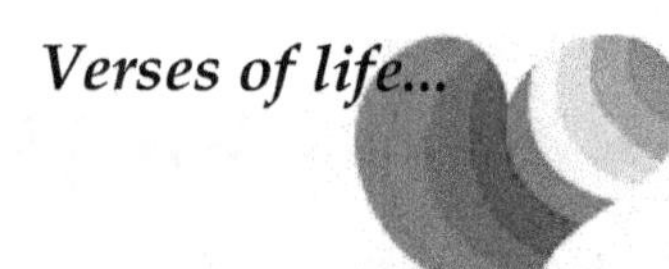

Verses of life...

Matthew 7:7 NKJV

As one of the powerful countries approves the 1st Corona virus vaccine, some are quite skeptic and unease. The world has to see first before it believes. With this news, we all believe God gives wisdom to whoever is incharge of the vaccine. As we pray, "Ask, and it will be given to you; seek, and you will find; knock, and it will be opened to you."

Rainbow Hues

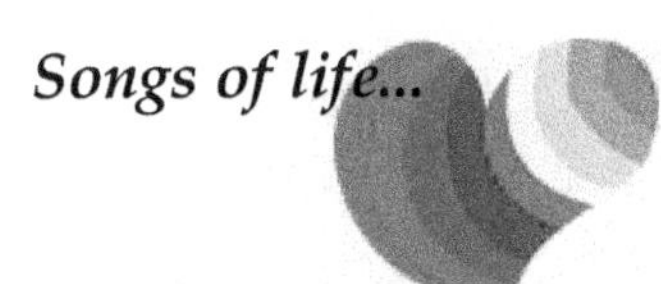

Lead Me, Lord

If God didn't give us what we prayed for, that's for our protection and direction. Don't get discouraged. Let God lead us to the right path. Yes, we will stumble and fall to make us strong. But, we will not go astray. God will surely lead us from sunrise to sunset. And we all sing, Lead me, Lord.

Rainbow Hues

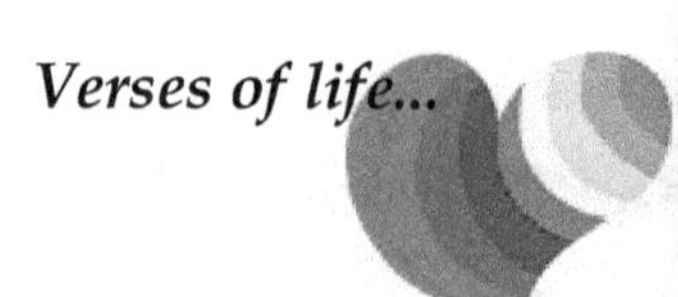

Verses of life...

Psalm 25:5 ESV

In a world where survival of the fittest exists, we all want (whether we admit it or not) to lead our own lives. We don't care how others lead their lives. We even lie just to win the race of life. We have to acknowledge that God is in control and he's here to lead. As we pray, "Lead me in your truth and teach me, for you are the God of my salvation; for you I will wait all the day long."

Rainbow Hues

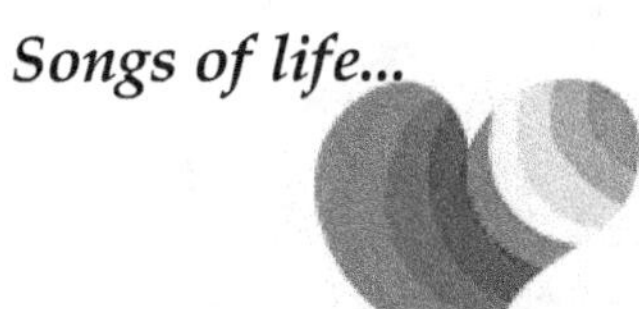

God will make a Way

When life is filled with darkness and there seems to be no way, call on God's help. He will make away to safely pass by these muddy and rocky roads. If the way is unclear and life is uncertain, God is walking beside us. Be brave and walk on. Keep going. And we all sing, God will make a way.

Rainbow Hues

Verses of life...

John 14:6 NLT

If we only lead our lives in accordance of God's will, life will not become complicated. Challenging times will always be there. However, God is always there too to prepare the way for us. Through Him, life will find its way. Words become true. Our way is clear and certain. As we pray, "Jesus told him, "I am the Way, the Truth and the Life. No one can come to the Father except through me."

Rainbow Hues

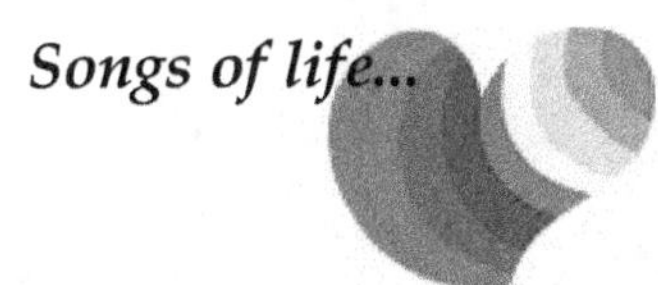

Natutulog Ba Ang Diyos?

Trials come in different forms and sizes. As they say the hardest battles are given to the strongest soldiers. Life may seem unfair. We keep on comparing why others' lives are good and ours are full of storms. With our own understanding, we thought God abandons us. And we all sing,'Wag mo sanang akalaing Natutulog pa ang Diyos?.

Rainbow Hues

Verses of life...

Jeremiah 23:23 GNT

Burdens we shoulder today will be the blessings we enjoy someday. God sees our struggles in life. The tests of life we are facing. The crosses we are carrying. The sufferings we are enduring. The sacrifices we are going through. God knows our pains. God has witnessed all these. As we pray, "I am a God who is everywhere and not in one place only."

Rainbow Hues

Songs of life...

Lift Up Your Hands

We face adversities but not every day. Bad days are part of someone's life. We feel tired, exhausted, drained and hopeless. This, too, shall pass. Despite all these hardships in life, life is still a blessing to be thankful for. And we all sing, Lift up your hands to God, and He'll make you feel all right.

Rainbow Hues

Verses of life...

Matthew 11:28 NIV

Rest but never quit. Take a break but don't give up. Let your tears flow. Cry until the pain disappears. Talk to God. Tell Him all your heartaches. Allow God to comfort you with His loving arms. As we pray, "Come to me, all you who are weary and burdened, and I will give you rest."

Rainbow Hues

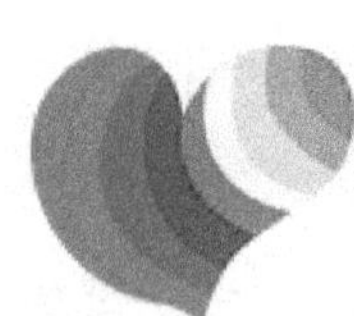

Disclaimer: Image not mine / cttro

*Lift up your hands to God, and He'll make you feel
all right*

3 WORDS TO FOREVER

WORDS LEFT UNSAID

WORDS ARE POWERFUL

Words can either make or break a person. Whatever word we say to others or ourselves may happen to us. So, be constructive with your words. Choose them well. If you cannot keep quiet, atleast be careful with your choice of words.

3 WORDS TO 4EVER...

Acknowledgement of God's goodness, self-affirmation and self-acceptance are three traits one should develop until it becomes a habit and part of his/her everyday life. These are words left unsaid, unspoken, undeclared and unexpressed.

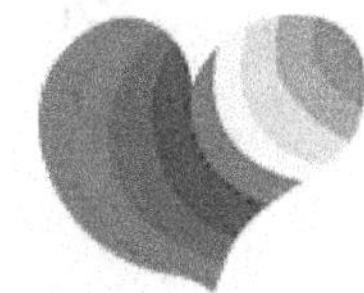

3 WORDS TO 4EVER...

I AM

Proudly State Your Name 7 times

As the saying goes, calling you by name is the sweetest music you can ever hear. Self-affirmation is unknowingly taken for granted by comparing oneself to others with the phrase, 'Sana All'.

WORDS LEFT UNSAID...

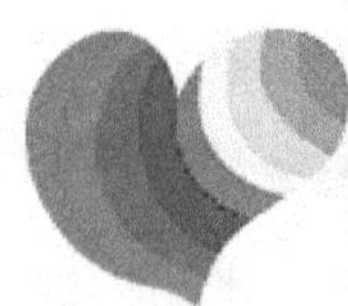

3 WORDS TO 4EVER...

I'M A
MASTERPIECE

God created you in His image and likeness. You are His work of art, creatively and meticulously done. Beautifully made!

3 WORDS TO 4EVER...

I AM IMPORTANT

Born poor or rich, it doesn't really matter. In God's eyes, you are as important as others. You are worthy.

WORDS LEFT UNSAID...

3 WORDS TO 4EVER...

I AM
CHOSEN

Many are called but few are chosen. Be proud, you are chosen to do great things and make things happen.

WORDS LEFT UNSAID...

3 WORDS TO 4EVER…

I AM PRECIOUS

You are a gem so precious. God takes care and watches over you. Remember that!

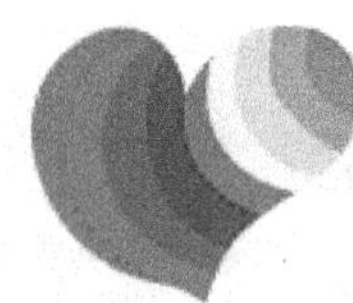

3 WORDS TO 4EVER...

I AM
LOVED

God is love. You live to love and to be loved. If you feel unloved, remember God loves you.

WORDS LEFT UNSAID…

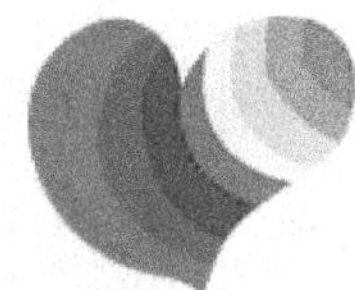

3 WORDS TO 4EVER...

I AM
be-You-tiful

Inside out you are beautiful.
Just being You, the true You
makes you one. Stay beautiful.

WORDS LEFT UNSAID...

3 WORDS TO 4EVER...

I AM
IRREPLACEABLE

You have your our own niche in this world. Your mark is different from others. You have your own place.

WORDS LEFT UNSAID...

3 WORDS TO 4EVER...

I AM
STRONG

Whatever storm that comes your way, you can face it. You are resilient more than you can imagine. Your spirit never gives up.

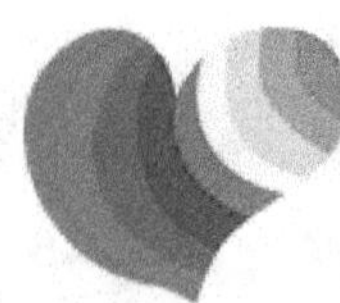

3 WORDS TO 4EVER...

I AM
TREASURED

God keeps you. He cherishes you. You are a treasure with priceless value. Take good care of yourself.

3 WORDS TO 4EVER...

I AM BLESSED

Life is a blessing. You are favored. You are fortunate. You are blessed to be a blessing to others.

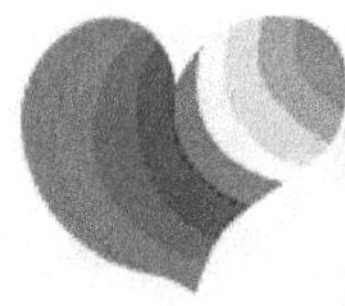

3 WORDS TO 4EVER...

I AM
UNFORGETTABLE

Every day is your moment. Seize the day. Create memories that will last. Make that moment and you hard to forget.

WORDS LEFT UNSAID

3 WORDS TO 4EVER...

I AM
CAPABLE

You have the ability to make things work. God gives you strength to produce beautiful results.

3 WORDS TO 4EVER...

I AM ENOUGH

You are good enough to make
a positive change in this world.
God has gifted you with skills
and talents to show the world
what you have got.

WORDS LEFT UNSAID...

3 WORDS TO 4EVER...

I AM ORIGINal

You are not a copy-cat. You are not a second rate. You are unique. No one can be You because you are you.

3 WORDS TO 4EVER...

I'M NOT PERFECT

Self-Acceptance is a way of acknowledging our imperfections, and recognizing our flaws that we are humans. Humans who can not do everything but can do something. Our weaknesses remind us to be humble.

WORDS LEFT UNSAID...

3 WORDS TO 4EVER...

I'M (NOT) OKAY

It is okay to admit that you are not okay. Not everyday is a good day. Not everybody is always okay. You have to process until you recover from it.

3 WORDS TO 4EVER...

I'M (NOT) POWERFUL

You may be powerless in other aspects. But you have the power to inspire, to touch lives and the power to make a difference. Use your power that shines within.

WORDS LEFT UNSAID...

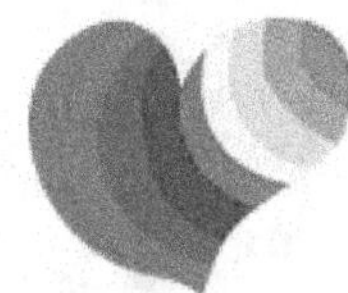

3 WORDS TO 4EVER…

I'M (NOT) ALONE

You are never alone.
Somebody thinks of you.
Somebody prays for you. God
will never forsake nor abandon
you. God is with you 'till the
end of time.

WORDS LEFT UNSAID…

3 WORDS TO 4EVER...

MY LIFE MATTERS

You matter. Your life does matter. Your words matter. Everything about you matters. Never waste it for nothing. God created You for a purpose.

WORDS LEFT UNSAID...

3 WORDS TO 4EVER...

MAGICAL WORDS

These are considered basic and simple words yet taken for granted. These leave indelible marks in the hearts of the receiver. These words are so magical. These build harmonious relationships and open doors of friendships. Respect, Peace and Encouragement are some of the messages conveyed in saying these pleasant words.

WORDS LEFT UNSAID...

3 WORDS TO 4EVER...

Please, Kindly, May I

These words start a request statement. It has always been pleasant to hear a request that starts with polite words. Using these gives respect to someone who will do the favor.

3 WORDS TO 4EVER...

I
Thank
You

A simple thank you to someone who did something for you reminds him/her effort. The favor doesn't have to be big to receive a thank you message.

3 WORDS TO 4EVER...

I
Appreciate
You

Appreciating someone for what he did reminds him/her goodness. It doesn't matter if the act is big or small. A small act of kindness should be appreciated and valued.

3 WORDS TO 4EVER...

I
Am
Sorry

Pride forbids us to say these three simple words. Saying these words seems the hardest thing to do. However, if your heart knows how to forgive, saying sorry becomes part of your life.

WORDS LEFT UNSAID...

3 WORDS TO 4EVER...

I
Love
You

When was the last time you said I Love You? Let your loved ones know how much you love them. Make saying I Love You a habit. Time is passing by. We are growing old. Before it will be too late, Say I Love You often to your family and friends.

WORDS LEFT UNSAID...

3 WORDS TO 4EVER...

GOD IS GOD

I could never imagine a life without God. Life without God is meaningless and colorless. I talk about Him even though I haven't seen Him.

This is because I believe in Him. I thank Him for His grace and blessings. I am grateful for His undying love. I praise Him for all the great things He has done for me. I worship Him for all the amazing things He has shown me.

I always trust in Him with or without storms in life. I hold on to His promises. My hope is in Him. He is faithful. He is a God of all.

God is love. He gave His only begotten Son to save us from our sins. He first loved us because we are His children.

God is joy. He makes all things beautiful. He is the joy that lasts forever. Our happiness doesn't depend on people or things. The joy of knowing Him is more than enough.

God is our protector. God protects us from any harm. He lets us live our lives with His protection from any evil acts.

God is our light in darkness. He doesn't allow anyone to live in darkness. He doesn't let us to stumble and fall.

God is our strength. Philippians 4:13, I can do all things through Christ who strengthens me.

God is our all. God is our everything. Psalm 23, The Lord is my shepherd: I shall not want.

God is good all the time. All the time, God is good.

WORDS LEFT UNSAID...

3 WORDS TO 4EVER...

Note: Image not mine / cttro

God's with us! Keep the Faith!

WORDS LEFT UNSAID...

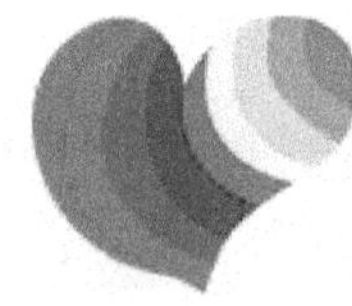

RAINBOW GAZERS

COLORFUL STORIES OF WAGI

Where a Rainbow Story becomes a Colorful Testimony

W - omen
A - re
G - reat
I - influencers

There are many featured Rainbow stories of Champion Women who made difference in their chosen fields. Some of them are Miriam Defensor Santiago (1st Asian elected ICC judge), Jaclyn Jose (1st Filipino Cannes Best Actress), Catriona Gray (1st Filipina represented PH at Miss World & Miss Universe), Angel Locsin (1st Filipina Actor included in the list of Forbes Asia's Heroes of Philanthrophy) to name a few.

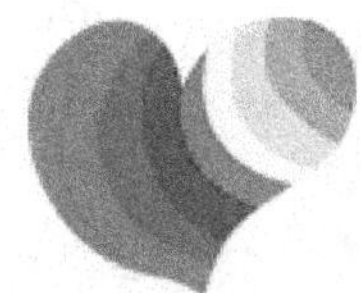

WAGI...

BORN, MADE, AND CALLED TO LEAD AND SERVE

They say leaders are either born or made. In the case of this leader, she was both. She was born to be a leader. Her leadership was because of "nature and nurture". Leadership was in her genes and natural makeup and this was even nurtured further through the many opportunities given to her to lead.

She was the eldest among eight children in the family. Being such, she was expected to be the leader. She was the co-leader of her parents ever since she was young. She was the "other parent" in the family. Her words were orders and laws to her siblings. She was always reminded by her parents that being the eldest in the family, it was required of her to always be good because her siblings look up to her. It was a tough responsibility to be the eldest.

Throughout her growing years, she gave her best to be a good sister because she knew that she has significance in the formation of her siblings. She was their "other parent." Upon entering school, she brought with her the leadership trait borne along with her being the eldest. However, it was different at school. She was no longer the eldest. In fact, she was the youngest. She was Grade 1 at the age of five. It would have been difficult for her to lead, but she became the leader of the class even if she was the youngest. She was even called the "Small Teacher". She may be the smallest and thinnest in class and yet she was the brightest. She was both her classmates' classmate and teacher, and was always requested by her teachers to tutor her classmates struggling in reading and mathematics. When she graduated in elementary, it was her that gave the valedictory speech.

During high school, she studied in a private Catholic school where everyone was a scholar because their education was funded and supported by a foundation. And although she was again the youngest among her classmates, it never deterred her from achieving. She strenuously gave her best entitling her the

leader in the class. She was active in both academics and extracurricular activities.

She also began serving her community and parish. Molding her to develop not only academically but also spiritually and even having social responsibility. She learned Christian values and tried her best to live up to it.

Her family was in deep poverty that it would be impossible to send her to college. Thanks to the school's Program for college scholarships. She availed of this and took the examination. She was blessed to have passed the requirements and the processes and was awarded with a college scholarship. She successfully hurdled the demands of the scholarship which included a rendering of a 60-hour service in the College library or any office and met the required general average. It was noteworthy to add the fact that the college she was at, was exclusive for rich girls. While she was in that College, she never forgot her roots as well, inspiring her to reach her dream of finishing her studies. She was a volunteer catechist in a public high school and a teacher in the College's Night Secondary School. It taught her to value the importance of blending work with prayer. During her college years, our country regained freedom from dictatorship. She then realized that by becoming an empowered woman, she can contribute to the growth of the country.

When she started teaching, she brought with her all the values she learned from her family and schools. She taught grade school-kids in private school for first three years and another six years to high school students in her Alma Mater. After serving the private schools for a total of nine years, she transferred to a public school. She excelled as a Teacher. And she was not only good for teaching Science, but also a good friend and parent to the students. After teaching for nine years, she was promoted to an administrative position as a Head Teacher and Principal.

Her was first assigned as School Head in a poor coastal community school which was always ravaged by floods. But despite having this challenge, she embraced it. She did not only stay in her office focusing on her mandates as a principal but wholeheartedly served beyond what was required for her. She enhanced and applied her networking skills and looked for partners to support the students, the school, and the community. By engaging the community and other stakeholders, she was admirably able to transform the school into a performing school. She taught the learners the courage to chase their dreams after high school and that motivated her to partner with universities for their scholarships. She paid forward as a scholar herself.

She also contributed to the coastal communities by actively participating in their disaster risk management programs. She was enthusiastically involved with the Mangrove Reforestation Program of the school and the community. She immersed herself in the community, hence, becoming one of them.

Her next assignment as a Principal was a huge school. She was faced with another challenge, to lead and supervise more than 100 teachers and 3000 learners. Amazingly, she engaged, enabled, and empowered the teachers. She mentored them to become quality teachers for their learners. Yes, she was able to transform the school into a School of Champions.

After being a School Head, she was called and was anointed to a higher position. She became the leader of leaders. It was again a challenge for her to lead former bosses and colleagues. But she faced it, even exerting her best in serving. She contributed to the organization's transformation in terms of improved processes. Initiating innovations focused on human resource development, resource management, strategic planning, and, partnership and collaboration. She advocated for Mayap Leadership which means being a good steward, shepherd, and servant leader. This was visibly learned through her examples. For her, being a leader is a calling from God; hence, she was accountable to the people she serves and to God who anointed her to be a leader. As a leader, she should always bring the light that guides wherever she was sent to lead and serve. She always vows to SHINE - Serve, Heal, Inspire, Nurture, and Empower,

and through this, she makes the face of the Lord, Who called her to lead and serve, shine. She was always grateful for being born, made, and called to be a servant leader.

Written by: Rowena T. Quiambao

Rainbow Gazers...

MAKING TODAY MATTER

"Things happen for a reason, we may never understand why and how they exist, trust God and He will help you get through it."

Be Aware
"The first step toward change is awareness. The second step is acceptance."
-Nathaniel Branden

Sometime in 2018, Kaye noticed a small lump in her right breast. She then went to see her ob-gyn for consultation. The doctor associated it with the menstrual cycle and breastfeeding. For her to make sure the ob-gyn referred her to a surgeon for further check-up. That year, Kaye's worries were answered. She had seen an oncologist too in Pasig to make sure.

In 2019, the surgeon decided to remove the lump unfortunately while she was in the operating room, Kaye's cough was so intense that they could not proceed to the operation. Until the pandemic happened, no reschedule of operation was done due to hectic schedules too.

Later this June of 2020, Kaye noticed that the lump grew and decided to see her surgeon again. The surgeon then scheduled her for a core needle biopsy before any operation.
Just before the doctor had seen the result, Kaye made some research already upon fetching the result from the diagnostics laboratory.

Note: Please be aware and concern about whatever you feel in your body.

The Shocking Truth
"Truth will make you cry and stumble but it will be a way to ease the pain afterward."

Kaye and her husband went to see the surgeon for the result's interpretation and the surgeon confirmed that Kaye has breast cancer, and it was invasive. Kaye's reaction was unpredictable because she heard it and it was clear. Her husband sitting beside her was so

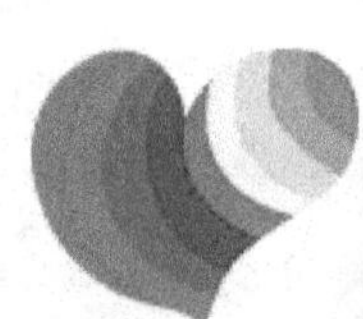

helpless during that time. Tears fell from their eyes; the doctor's eyes were even teary.

Then at the doorstep, her husband hugged her so tight while both of them cried. Who would have thought that it would happen, right?

They rode on the way quietly while tears ran down their eyes. Both were praying for strength that they might get through this challenge.

They told their mediate family members and relatives about it. Kaye's concern was how to tell them, because she was afraid that they can't accept it that easily especially her mother.

Love Tank is Full

"Love is always bestowed as a gift - freely, willingly and without expectation. We don't love to be loved; we love to love."

-Leo Buscaglia.

Since that day, Kaye's life changed. What do you expect for someone learning that she has cancer? Shut themselves out of the world, cry to death, curse God, question God, hate the world, or even themselves. God is so good that

Kaye was strong and was courageous. Jesus pulled that dagger of pain in her heart and replaced it with love.

Kaye received a lot of prayers from her family, relatives, and colleagues. These make her battle a lot lighter. Now, she began to experience life through a different lens, becoming more empathetic and more spiritually in tune. The support of her children, husband, mother, sister, family, and friends kept her going during this difficult time.

Acceptance
"The first step toward change is awareness. The second step is acceptance."
-Nathaniel Branden

Kaye's situation was unbelievable. However, she accepted her present state. She did not even question God, why would she? Never did she blame anyone for it. Kaye believes that accepting one's dilemma or struggle makes a lot of difference. For her, sulking herself in a room or feeling miserable for herself will not make any difference nor may help her state. Why would she make herself miserable, if she can use it for something that God may have a purpose for? It may be hard for you to believe because she cannot believe how strong she has become. She needs to be strong for her children. They are one of her deepest Whys' not to give up. A very supportive and loving husband is always there for her; her mother who has always been there for her, for them, and her loving sister who has been so concern. God is with her in this battle. That's what she believes and her faith is strong. God is her healer.

Prayer

P-ay attention to God's intentions

R-emind yourself consistently, God loves you

A-ffirm yourself always, God is with you

Y-earn to God's awesome blessings

E-ncourage others to be a blessing too

R-est, pray, cry, surrender, forgive, and talk to God.

HE listens.

Faith-Hope-Love

"And now these three remain faith, hope and, love. But the greatest of these is love."
Corinthians 13:13

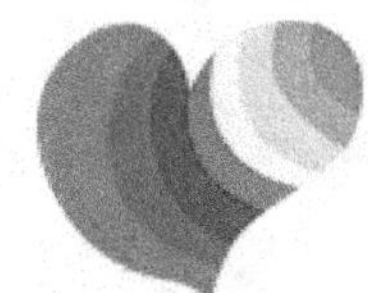

Kaye created a page on her Facebook "Faith-Hope-Love". Her purpose in creating the page is to spread positivity, faith, hope and, love through quotes, videos, and the like. She shares her journey too, on this page. That is for awareness especially for women. Her oncologists said that most of the patients that she handles are teachers like her. May this page be part of your daily motivations and may it cuddles you in your most trying hours. Just like the lines from the song, "True Colors". *"I see you true color that's why I love you, so don't be afraid to let them show, your true color, true color is beautiful like a rainbow."*

You can visit, like, share and be part of her page https://www.facebook.com/F8HopeLuv Her Message:

She never expects herself to be so ready. She expects herself to cry, because this is one of the things she has to deal with. Constant self-assurance and strong faith to God made her feel so light. Acceptance makes a difference. It does matter.

She may never know how and what kind of difficulty you are going through right now, it's okay to cry. Sometimes one must be mindful of

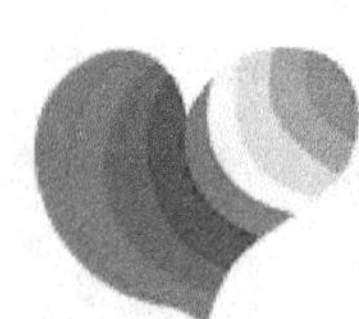

his/her emotions. Let go of your guard...it's totally fine.

Once you're done releasing it, compose yourself and ask God for directions. HIS response may not be that immediate... NEVER WORRY BEFORE YOU EVEN CONSULTED HIM, GOD KNOWS IT ALREADY. TRUST HIM, HE KNOWS EVERYTHING.
Make every day count. Make today count.
Praying and claiming blessings of a healthy mind, body, and spirit for everyone.

Written by: Catheryn E. Reyes

Rainbow Gazers…

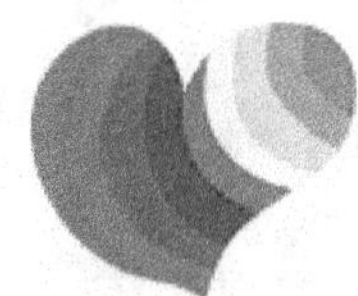

WAGI...

Silver Lining of Motherhood

There are times that people who are not even really close to her will approach her and, *"You know you have a great son, unlike the other youth of his age he seems to be very formal, respectful, and disciplined."* She feels elated, and will utter to herself, *"I did a great job."*

As she looks back to her beginning as a mother , it was like a roller coaster. She conceived her son when she was working abroad after the miscarriage of her first pregnancy. She was still traumatized with that event when her OB-Gyn informed her that a certain hormone is being secreted slightly higher than it should be. She was advised to take a laboratory test that would check if he's genetically complete by taking amniotic fluid directly from her womb. (She has phobia with needles). While waiting for the result, her OB had started counseling her and her husband of a possibility to abort him. What if the findings are that her son is mentally retarded has Down syndrome or physically handicapped? Asking herself, "Are we willing to sacrifice ourselves to have him for the rest of our lives?" She felt devastated; she even asked her OB if there is something wrong with her? Is she not worthy to be a mother?

14 long days, sleepless nights, contemplating, and acceptance of her son regardless of the result. Abortion was never an option for her, thanks for the kind of culture she was brought by her parents. When the genetics revealed that he has complete chromosomes and they have nothing to worry, no one can imagine the feeling she had.

She was on her 40th week and a day when she had her last appointment with her OB before delivery. It was 8 pm of Wednesday that she started spotting; they went to the hospital the next day. She had labor the whole time, those painful contractions had nurses, and doctor offered her to have painless delivery, which she gladly rejected. She wanted to feel her baby welcoming this world. It was good that she has high tolerance to pain but not with needles, ironically though.

It was Friday at 3:35 am that she successfully delivered him. Tears swelled from the mix emotions when she finally saw him. However, her body had not expelled the placenta right away. According to the books she read, it would normally come almost the same time with the baby or until about 45 minutes after the delivery. She had already slept for about an hour from exhaustion when she suddenly felt that she was being sucked downward and literally swirling that she suddenly grasp to hold onto something. She felt that she was falling so fast and screaming for someone to help and get hold of her. She felt she was dying but she must not, not yet, she wanted to stay with her son. Luckily, her husband was beside her and pushed the emergency button and in instant, she had medical staffs around her. The placenta was manually taken from inside of her and they stitched her episiotomy without anesthesia. It was extremely painful that she thought she would never again have pregnancy.

The government of the foreign country they are in forbids the stay of foreign family. They had planned that she and her son will go back to the Philippines and her husband will move to United Kingdom, then she will join him later and finally petition their son. It was a great plan. With her son they went back home, they stayed with her in-laws for two years.

The plan of joining him never happened. She was able to acquire a small parcel of land in a place nearer her family and they moved there. This is where they live now. It was only four months when somebody phoned her that her husband is having an affair. She was brokenhearted; she can't sleep, eat, drink and go on with her life. She even thought of killing herself but then seeing her son she doesn't want to leave him. He was only three years old then. So she thought she would kill him then kill herself. She was very shattered. She learned to drink until she was wasted for only then she forgets what is happening.

There were times that all the people were sleeping and she was still awake crying her heart out. By the day, she would bring her son with her and spent the whole day at malls. She did not want to be alone. She was depressed. She had to do something. She was afraid of her thoughts, so she sent her son to Day Care institution and she went to study a technical course. She met new friends and they introduced her to Born Again Christian living. She was renewed and reborn in spirit. She was able to see things in new perspective. All along God gave her a son to be her strength to keep on living. He is her silver lining. She was able sort her life back. She sought employment to provide her son's need better.

She was a substitute teacher then and taking master's degree at the same time, when her son was diagnosed with Attention Deficit Hyperactive Disorder (ADHD). She stopped her schooling and led her son to his therapy as his medication comes first. Through seminar, she was educated about his standing. It was not easy to accept it but she told herself it was just the two of them. No one will better understand him except her. With better perspective in life and seeing her son as her silver lining, they're able to accept it. He was six years old then and had continuous medication until aged nine. There were instances that she was sought by his teachers due to short attention span, inattentiveness, impulsiveness, unruliness, short-tempered, fidgety, tantrums, he tore his classmates' things, he smashed the blackboard and many more but she took a pause and attended to bidding. Telling herself, *"I will never turn my back on him."* What he got was something he never wished, and what he had done may never be his intentions. She firmly stands to support and guide her son for God lends him to her as a covenant of His love. Their relationship may not be perfect; there are times that they provoke each other.

They fight, scream, cry, frustrate but they also enjoy, bond, do the road trip, the food trip and most of all love and accept both their shortcomings.

With the roller coaster they are in, she sometimes asked herself, *"Am I doing the right thing as a solo parent? Am I not being too much or too lenient*

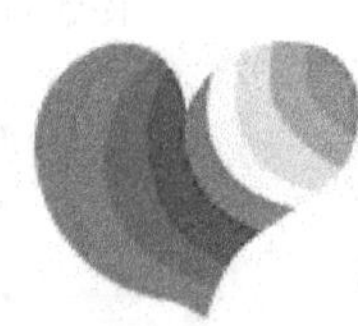

in disciplining him. He is now 17 years old and still a lot of years ahead of us."

With faith and trust, God is with them and they will be able to fit in whatever life throws them.

Written by: Teckles Sweet

Rainbow Gazers...

WAGI...

Small but Terrible!

In this competitive world, it is not always the gifted ones in height that lead and reign. As the saying goes, "Height doesn't matter!"
This is a David-like story of a woman who has surpassed trials in her life that she too could not ever imagine how she has conquered her own game in the so called life.

Life is a game that requires an enormous amount of mental and physical efforts as they say. Inevitably, the world is a jungle, and that the ignoble ones are at the bottom of the food chain.

For her, life is as simple as she needs to eat three times a day. Lucky if she can have meals three times within a day. Her strong will to transform her life from this kind of situation has enabled to overcome all the pains and hardships in the battle. With family, her struggle to eat three times a day ended through her perseverance and hard work.

Now, as she reaches the apex of her education knowing that she worried it when she was in high school, she can finally say, She is really a "small but terrible."

If one has a strong desire to transform life and willing to achieve for it, this person is more likely to succeed. For her, hard work and perseverance served as her passport to success. But it is not proper to commend one's own achievements, so she'd asked her colleagues what makes her really a "Small but terrible" woman.

"-with her small hands, she is able to accomplish big things as she multitasks."
"-with her small eyes, she can see bigger possibilities and potentials in different situations and people."
"-with her small body, she can endure even the most pressing situations."

Teaching in a public school tests a teacher's patience and resiliency. It is essential in dealing the day-to-day challenges of managing their own classroom, with colleagues and the

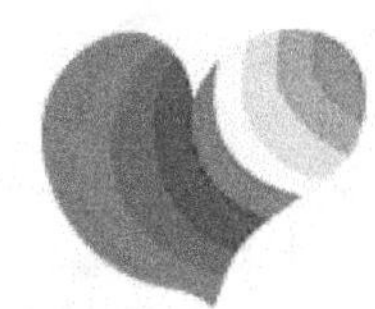

community. They spend eight (8) hours daily in working all for the success of the school.

As she entered teaching in 2007, handled 6 teaching loads and she was given an opportunity to work in the operation of the school by staying in the principal's office and helping Head Teachers with their jobs. These added tasks required her to stay more than 8 hours official time in the school. But to no regrets, the learning opportunity given to her was her training ground to develop her managerial skills. Sooner or later as they foresee her to become a school head in the near future (with her fingers crossed).

As she performs her duties as a teacher, she was also a student. At first, they all pushed her to enroll in the higher education because it was a requirement for a managerial position. She was hesitant to enroll at first, because of the pressure she received from her colleagues. In the end as she went to school every Saturday and even Sunday attending Ed.D.class, she managed to finish the apex of her education career. It gave her an extra sense of accomplishment as a person.

Another reason, she was enjoying her life and roles as wife and a mother. Her energy boosted in performing her duties as a teacher and a student because of her family source of inspiration. She feels great everytime she captures opportunities and grows in the workplace. Her husband and kids' love serves as her wind beneath her wings and her fuel to do well every day. She has never got tired in providing for her family.

Like other notable women in history whose height has never been a hindrance to shine the brightest in their chosen career, this petite woman has proven that height doesn't always matter.

With sheer determination, hard work, good work ethics, and positive attitude in life, nothing is impossible to find one's worth and find a place under the sun.

Written by: Cyrell Q. Galang

Rainbow Gazers...

WAGI...

Fair Share of Rainbow Story

There are many aspects of her life that she would like to share and how a rainbow (figuratively) became associated with them. But for the meantime, let her share this one.

Ever since she was a little kid, she always dreamt of being in front of a class, teaching. She thought to herself that being able to impart her knowledge and skills to students is a lifelong dream. Though, back in 1999, she was contemplating which course to enroll to. During that time, computer-related courses were in demand, so she enrolled in BS Computer Science. For four years, she learned many things especially in programming. She knew that it was not her cup of tea, but good thing, she was able to pass her subjects pretty well.

After graduation, she was able to work in different companies as HR Timekeeper, HR Encoder, then HR Recruitment and Training

Personnel. She enjoyed her job, but little did she know that the Lord had a bigger plan. In 2007, she was hired as a college instructor in a small school in Quezon City. There she taught English and Computer related subjects. She had students who were in her age, while some were younger. During her course of teaching, she must say that she really enjoyed teaching them, not only in terms of academic subjects, more so about life. That was the very point in her life that she said to herself, "*I love teaching*". Then came 2009, she was given the opportunity to teach in a newly established school in Minalin, Pampanga. She handled computer subjects and did office tasks, too. In 2013, she was employed in a bigger school offering Junior High as Department Coordinator. Yes, she loves teaching, but that was not enough. She was negatively judged to handle the position because she was not a BSEd graduate. There was even a point that due to an upcoming accreditation, the management had to change her position in all documents from coordinator to teacher. At first it was not a big deal for her, however, the turning point compelled her to take units in Methodology in Teaching. Then years later, she took some units in Master of Education in Educational Management (she has not finished yet). And until now, she is engaged in the academe.

Twice, she took the Licensure Examination for Teachers, due to her bachelor's degree, she is under the Mathematics major in which she has neither formal training nor exposure...eventually, she failed. She thought, maybe teaching was not really for her. Maybe she can be passionate about it, but having a license is still a big thing. She thought of quitting teaching and applies for a different job; however, it was not the case. The more she resisted, another teaching opportunity comes in.

This time, she finally realized that God has been guiding her in fulfilling her life's purpose, and that is to teach, to touch lives, and to be a blessing to others. She is not saying that a professional license in teaching is not important, but having a heart for teaching is far more important. She is blessed she gets to see big genuine smiles from her students:

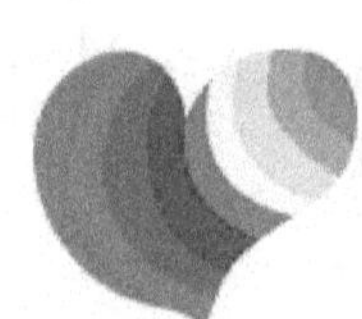

former and new, and telling her stories of their achievements become her achievements, too. They say that, *"There's a rainbow always after the rain"*, and she believes in that too. Apart from that, *"There is a pot of gold at the end of a rainbow."* As for her, she gets her fair share of pot of gold, her dear students.

Written by: Carol B. Briones

Rainbow Gazers...

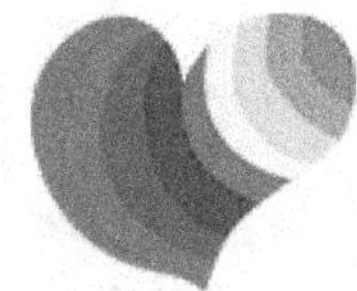

WAGI...

BORN WINNER

It has been14 years now since she became part of the teaching profession. In 2006, she graduated Bachelor of Science in Home Economics at Pampanga State Agricultural University (formerly Pampanga Agricultural College) in Magalang, Pampanga.

Actually, her ambition was not to become a teacher but to study MassCom in Manila. However, her family especially her mom had a problem financially; so she decided to have her college in Pampanga. She insisted that taking education course would ensure her stability in life. And she said, whatever course will offer on the first department in that school, she will grab it. Well, that was the time she saw the first department where all girls were in pink skirt. That was her story in College.

When she graduated, that was when she realized, she needs to embrace the fact that she will become a teacher. *(Wala ng urungan, wala ng sukuan!).* Being a teacher, her role will not finish in school, while she lives, she will always be a teacher.

She struggled more when she entered in public school as she encountered a mass number of students every day. She was not able to choose what subject she wants, whatever the principal wanted her to have, she goes on with that. She encountered difficulty with her co-workers as well, others were friends while some pretend to be friends, too. However, that does not mean, she hated them. Because she always said to herself, *"God always puts those people behind for you to gain courage, they are the spices in everyday menu"*.

As years go by, she experienced leaders that opposed her; however, God always reminds her *"submission is the great key"*. She did not expect that she would become a researcher that would present her study abroad. However, she loves to innovate and read books. On her career as teacher, planning, organizing, innovating was her greatest strength that was how she sees herself.

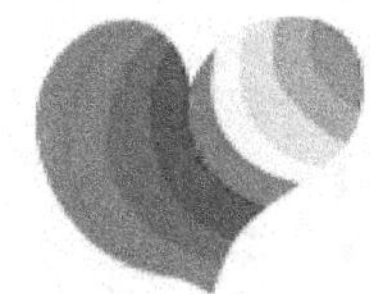

In 2011, she had encountered family problems wherein her mother had a hip injury and her father was sent to rehabilitation center because of alcoholism and while she was pregnant with her second child. She saw that her life was in a great despair.

In 2015, another life's test came, her mom was diagnosed with cancer. During that situation, her mother told her that she was an adopted daughter. She learned the truth at the age of 30. That truth did not upset her. She even took it positively and had no ill feelings towards her biological parents. She both prays for her adoptive and biological parents every day.

A great teacher must be a strong daughter and a mother too at the same time. That was how she thought that staying as a low rank teacher can't afford to sustain expenses. She prayed to God to help her in the situation. Months and a year passed, God became her great hope. He opened a door of opportunities, by having her own house with her complete family beside her and becoming the research coordinator of their school.

She has been exposed to the school system of management and leadership where she learned a lot. She met different people in the national and international scenarios. As she experienced those opportunities, her family was becoming supportive to her.

She also became active in their church services where she became a member of the worship team. That was how she gained encouragement and self-reflections on how God blesses her every day.

She studied books about educational science but her favorite book is the Bible where she always makes devotion and reflections guided with her course in theology at the Bible Training Center for Leaders and Pastors.

As she prays, *"If God plans me to become a master teacher, I will put my full trust in Him and always do my best."*

Written by: Pines Pangilinan

Rainbow Gazers...

WAGI...

KAY BUTI NG DIYOS

Lahat ng tao ay hindi naghangad kailanman na maisilang dito sa mundong ibabaw. Hindi nila pinili kung sino ang magiging mga magulang nila o kung sino ang kanilang magiging mga kapatid, bagkus tayo ay pinili ng Diyos, at pinili Niya tayong lahat sapagkat tayo ay mahalaga sa Kanya at dahil sa pag-ibig Niya nais Niyang ipakita ang napakagandang mundo na nilikha Niya para sa ating lahat.

Sa kwento ng may akda nito, alam niyang masayang-masaya ang Panginoong Diyos nang ilagay Niya siya sa sinapupunan ng kanyang ina. Alam Niya na siya ay lalaking isang guro.

Alam Niya kung saan siya dadalhin at alam din ng Panginoong Diyos kung ano ang mas nakakabuti para sa kanya. Pero ang tanong, bakit kaya siya nakakaranas ng mga pagsubok dito sa mundo yamang alam naman niyang Diyos ang nagdala sa kanya dito sa lupa? Maraming panalangin ang hindi rin nasasagot. Bakit kaya?
Dito sa lupa marami tayong pwedeng pagpilian, pinipili natin nang madalas ang mga bagay na sa palagay natin ay tama at dapat. Gayunman ang

mga pinipili natin minsan ay mga bagay na magaan, magaan sa lahat ng panahon.

Ayaw natin ng nabibigatan, ayaw nating makaranas ng kapighatian, pero bakit patuloy parin ang mga ganitong karanasan? Nananalig naman tayo sa Diyos, pero mas gusto pa rin kase natin ang mga bagay na nakakahiligan natin. Umiiyak pa nga tayo sa panalangin at humihingi ng ganito at ganyan, ngunit tayo at tayo parin ang nasusunod.

Mahal tayo ng Diyos, naniniwala din tayo sa Kanya, pero ipinagkakatiwala ba natin ang mga nais natin o sadyang tayo pa rin ang namimili ng mga gusto natin?

Minsan naitanong ng may akda sa kaniyang sarili kung ano ba ang pinakamabigat na desisyon na ginawa niya sa buhay. Ito ba yung pagpili nya ng kurso sa hinaharap? Ito ba'y tungkol sa kanyang magiging mga kaibigan o mga hindi niya dapat kaibiganin? O marahil sa pagpili ng magiging nobyo at magiging asawa balang araw?

Ang sagot niya sa sarili; "hindi", wala sa mga iyan ang maituturing na mabigat niyang desisyon. Ang pinakamabigat na pinili niya ay ang tangapin

ang Panginoong Hesus bilang sarili niyang tagapagligtas.

Ang sabi sa Juan 14 bersikulo 6 *"Sinabi ni Jesus sa kaniya: Ako ang Daan, ang Katotohanan at ang Buhay. Walang sinumang makakapunta sa Ama maliban sa pamamagitan ko."*

Pinanghawakan niya ang mga salitang iyan sa kanyang puso at hanggang sa mga oras na ito hindi niya pinagsisisihan na siya'y nilikha ng ating Panginoong Diyos. Hindi tayo pababayaan ng Diyos, hindi Niya tayo dadalhin sa mga kaguluhan at hinding-hindi Niya tayo iiwanan.

Kahit ano pa ang nagawa nating kamalian, ang mga kamay Niya ay patuloy paring nakagabay sa atin at nakatuon ang Kanyang mga mata sa atin. Mahal tayo ng Diyos. Sana'y paniwalaan natin na tayo ay nilikha Niya at hindi nagkamali ang mga magulang mo na ikaw ay naisilang dito sa mundo. Pinili ka Niya, at pinaisip din sa mga magulang mo ang napakagandang pangalan mo.

Remedios ang pangalan nang may akda, na magmula noong bata pa siya ay talagang pinakakinaiinisan niya. Pero nang makilala niya si Kristo bilang kanyang Diyos at tagapagligtas, natangap niya ang sarili bilang si Remedios M.

Santos na pinili ng Panginoong Diyos at nilikha Niya ayon sa Kanyang wangis.

Nagagalak siyang ipabatid sa atin lahat na anuman ang nararanasan natin ngayon ay walang kasalanan ang ating Diyos. Pinayagan Niya tayong pumili ng nais natin dahil mahal Niya tayo. Pero sana maunawaan natin na ang bawat desisyon ay may kaakibat na responsibilidad.

Kaibigan, kung sino ka man isa lang ang sasabihin ko, mahal ka ng Diyos. Mahal ka nang Diyos at higit sa lahat mahal na mahal tayo ng Diyos.

Maging masaya ano man ang mayroon tayo ngayon at kapag nakita nang Diyos ang puso natin na malinis at ibinibigay natin ang ating buhay sa Kanya, maniwala ka, pagpapalain ka Niya nang higit pa sa ninanais mo sa buhay!

Nagpapasalamat siya sa nararanasan niya sa kanyang buhay at dalangin niya na pagpalain tayong lahat ng Panginoong Jesus.

Isinulat ni Remedios M. Santos

Rainbow Gazers... ...

WAGI...

THE PARAGON of GAHEntados

The empowered woman behind Global Academy for Human Excellence is the Paragon of GAHEians, H.R.H. PROF. JOVYLYN S. ESPALABRA, D. HUM, D. LITT, Ph.D. She is the GAHEntado Founder and Chairman of GAHE founded in 2019.

Under her soaring wings are the Flock of Quintessential Personalities united in the name of World Peace and Humanity.

She is, indeed, the shining example of GAHEians for being a certified GAHEntado. Her depth and substance as a champion woman of life are best described through the four-letter acrostic word, GAHE:

G – lobal

She has many recognized active global affiliations and appointments. Two of these big chairwomanships are: She is the Secretary General of United Nations Economic and Social Council (UN ESC) and Global Chairman

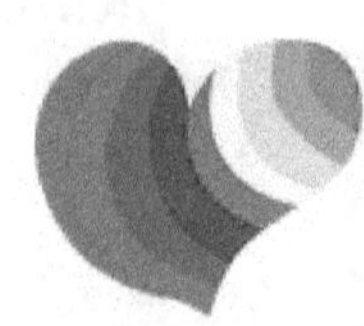

of Royal World Humanitarian Institution Kutai Mulawarman (RWHI-KM).

A – cademy

She is the Chairman of the Asia Pacific Region of Asian University International-Model United Nations (AUI-MUN). In 2019, AUI-MUN received the World Class Excellence award as the Most Innovative Global Education provider and Outstanding Global Honorary Doctoral Degree Provider awarded by Asia Pacific Awards Council.

H - uman

Being the mother of GAHE, she has modeled humanitarian activities in different aspects and social concerns such as education, peace, women empowerment, youth advocacy, and many others. Her heart, GAHE is a Global Humanitarian Institution Accredited Worldwide. This humanitarian organization is an advocate of peace, women and children's affairs and an advocate of education for all.

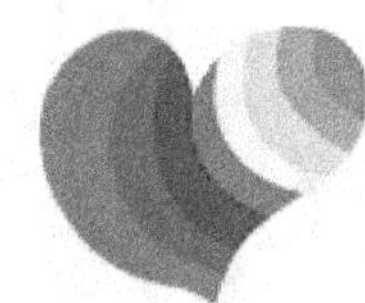

E – xcellence

Her hard work paid off. She was recognized as the 2019 World Class Achiever - Outstanding Asian Filipina Peace Advocate and Lady Entrepreneur by Asia Pacific Awards Council held in Malaysia.

Lifted from GAHE Fb page

Rainbow Gazers... ...

THE

GREAT

UNKNOWN

RAINBOW LIFE OF A TEACHER

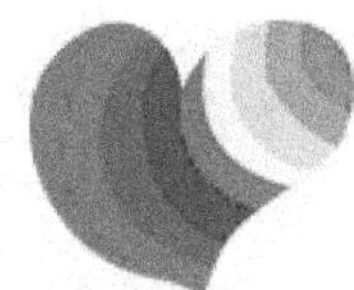

T – eachers should be

R - espected

E - levated

A - ppreciated and

T - reated well

Like you, teachers are humans who deserve encouragement and equal treatment.

Rainbow Life of a Teacher...

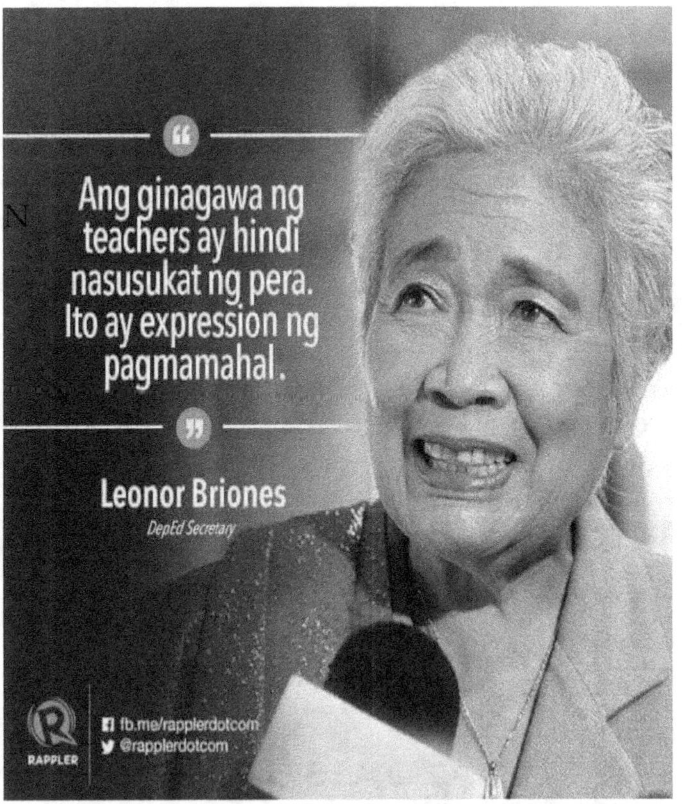

Disclaimer: Image not mine / credit to rappler

What the teachers do are, indeed, priceless!

Great Unknown...

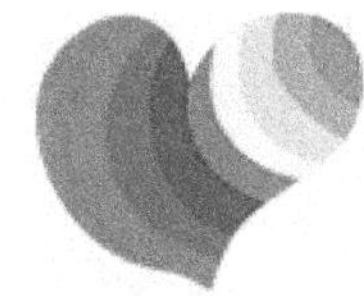

Rainbow Life of a Teacher...

Breaking News!

Opening of classes is deterred to Oct. 05 for SY 2020-2021.
Oct. 05 also commemorates World Teachers' Day.
This is the day where we do the TREAT (T-eachers should be R-espected, E-levated, A-ppreciated and T-reated well).
This new normal in education, may they receive the same treatment as they are doing their best working at home to be prepared and ready for students while you're relaxing well or sleeping soundly.

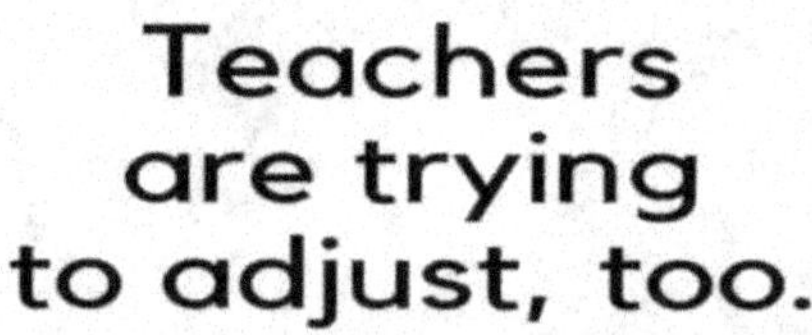

Disclaimer: Image not mine / cttro

Why should teachers be supported this new normal?

Great Unknown...

Rainbow Life of a Teacher...

Some discourteous people, now adays, can easily degrade and demoralize teachers without knowing their conditions and situations.

Teachers are humans, too. They have their own share of disaappointments, sacrifices, tears, rejections and sleepless nights. Rude people only see the shallow surface and outward appearance of what teachers are really doing every day. Teachers are, indeed, icebergs.

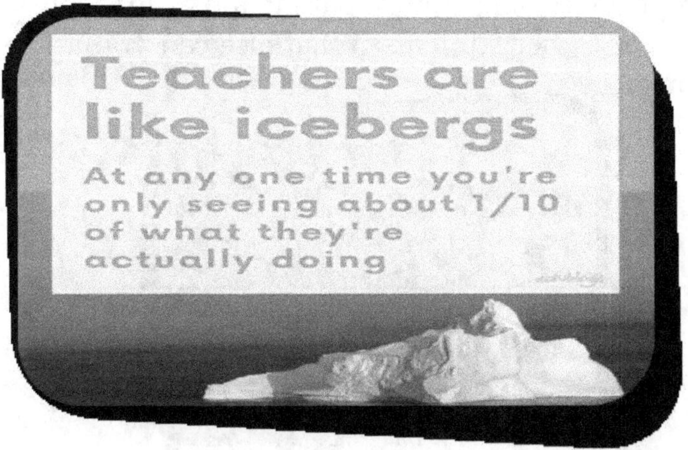

Disclaimer: Image not mine / cttro/edublogs

How much do you know about teachers and the roles they play?

Great Unknown...

Rainbow Life of a Teacher...

Disrespectful people with undeserving remarks against teachers obviously have no knowledge what the teachers do behind the camera. Teachers are one of the jack of all trades and master of all individuals who can do an unbelievable multi—tasking professional jobs.

Each day, they can be a social worker, health worker, an environmentalist, an agriculturist, an economist, and to name a few. Most importantly a biological parent and a surrogate parent to her students. What else can you ask for?

Disclaimer: Image not mine

How do teachers balancely paint their rainbow lives?

Great Unknown...

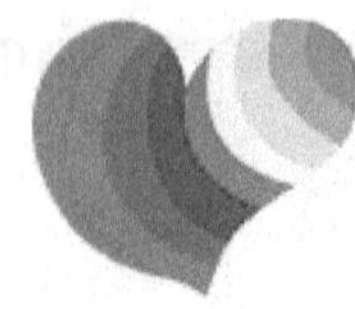

Rainbow Life of a Teacher...

Teachers' influence is forever. It lives in their students' lives. Successful or not, teachers will always have beautiful marks left in the hearts of their students.

As many always say, there will be no doctors, policemen, engineers, businessmen and other professions without the teachers. Teaching is still and will always be the mother of all professions.

Disclaimer: Image not mine / cttro

What makes teaching the noblest profession?

Great Unknown...

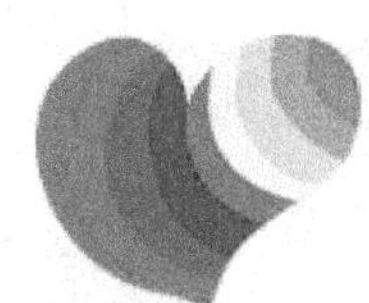

Rainbow Life of a Teacher...

Teachers are partners of parents in the holistic development of the students. Parents should understand how hard the job of the teachers. Teachers are not perfect. They do commit mistakes. They have flaws. Teachers' side should also be heard.

Disclaimer: Image not mine / cttro

Who will defend teachers when they become voiceless?

Great Unknown...

Rainbow Life of a Teacher...

Teachers are humans but their energy is beyond the 8 hours work. They are indefatigable. Weary Students draw strength from them. They also radiate light to their gloomy students. They are firm with their rules but their students have a soft spot in their hearts.

Disclaimer: Image not mine / cttro

How do teachers become rainbow in their students'
lives?

Great Unknown...

Rainbow Life of a Teacher…

Students usually come to school to learn. However, there are students who come to school to be accepted and loved. It is difficult for the students who have baggages in their lives to learn. It is hard for learning to take place if teachers teach only from the books.

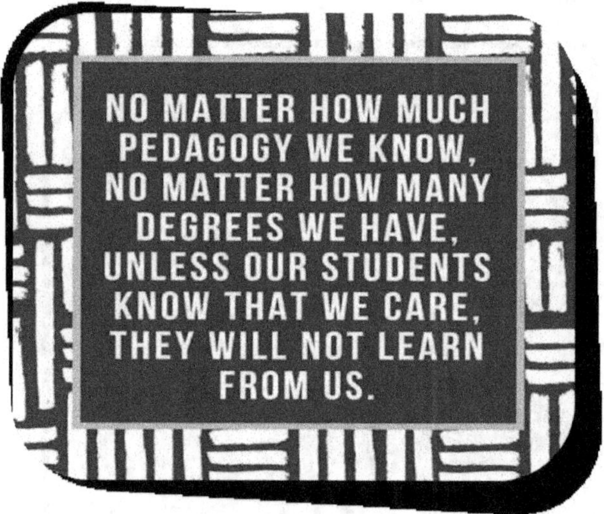

Disclaimer: Image not mine / cttro

When does learning really take place?

Great Unknown...

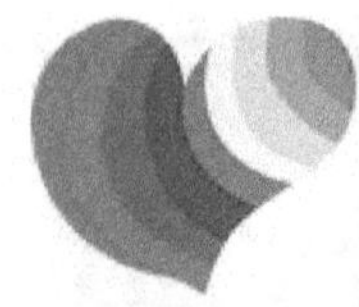

Rainbow Life of a Teacher...

Shaming be it physical, mental or digital should not be done to anyone. What does one get in bullying? in blaming? in shaming? Teachers didn't burn the midnight oil and acquire the license to teach just to be bullied, blamed and shamed. They are not only important part of the society. The future of the young ones lies in their hands. RESPECT!

Disclaimer: Image not mine / cttro

Why should teachers be protected from shaming?

Great Unknown...

Good Manners Right Conduct

Where Attitude not Aptitude defines your Altitude

Rainbow Life of a Teacher...

A MATENAKAN in the Truest Sense

A school is not only a learning venue for academics but a home of virtues. Though home is the primary source of education where magic words such as sorry, thank you, please are first learned from and taught by parents. Still, Schools are and will always be the second home that reinforce the values or sadly, first teach the good manners and right conduct not learned from home.

As an old adage says, "Values are caught not taught. Students as young as they are who experience much exposure on social media where words used and posts are not filtered give negative impressions that later on these young people imitate and manifest in their words and actions.

The students of this generation are so different from the previous ones. This has been observed by many, including teachers and psychologists.

A lot of old people often complain these days about how a lot of children are rude, disrespectful, and only think of themselves. Teachers are having a difficult time because their students have minds of their own and don't listen to what their educators are telling them to do.

Great Unknown...

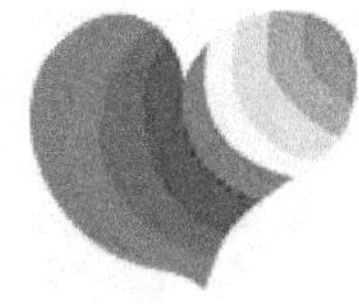

Rainbow Life of a Teacher...

Giant lack of R E S P E C T from students is a roaring grievance of teachers nowadays. Teachers clamor that respect for teachers must be first learned at home and taught by parents.

Disrespect, in the year of 2018, is another item added to the long list of cons--overcrowded class sizes. Incredibly low pay, mountain of paperworks-- of being a teacher and this one sits right at the top based on survey by Educator Quality of Work Life in 2017.

According to Noemi Moncada, Principal of Lagro National High School, many teachers are even bullied by parents of students who are subject to disciplinary action. The teachers are blamed for not teaching the kids what to do and how to behave, yet the parents forget that their children's values formation actually starts at home.

As reported by Buhay Guro, The Department of Education (DepEd) Region 2, Schools Division of Santiago City, recently earned praise from teachers after releasing a reminder to parents that learning about values and discipline should start at home.

In the memo, Division Superintendent of DepEd Santiago Dr. Florante Vergara reminded parents that it is at home that the children learn the foundation of good values and good manners, including how to be honest, diligent, and respectful.

Great Unknown...

Rainbow Life of a Teacher...

Students need to see their parents and guardians model and practice it in their everyday lives.

In view of this, the school adheres to DepEd's Core Values - **Maka-Diyos, Maka-tao, Makakalikasan and Makabansa.**

As per DepEd Order No. 8, s. 2015 on page 20, IV; the core values of the Filipino child be reflected in the report card. The core values have been translated into a behavior statement. In addition, indicators have been formulated for each behavior statement.

The teacher initiated a program on strengthening the Core Values Formation called **MATENAKAN WAY**

Eventually, through this program, most if not all as constant seekers of knowledge will always observe being Maka-Diyos, Maka-tao, Makakalikasan and Makabansa.

It takes a village to raise and educate a child. Holistic Development of a child needs not only parents neither the teachers alone. It takes a whole community to produce a good person.

Partnership of parents is the vital part of a successful program. Home and school should work hand in hand where parents model the values and teachers reinforce them. Constant monitoring is a must. Merely being reactive

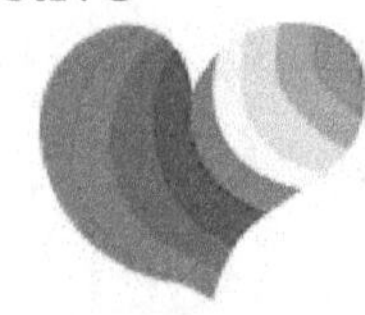

will not achieve the target goal. Every teacher is advised to proactively

implement the program. Concrete manifestation of core values is highly advised among students particularly those who are observed rude and disrespectful.

With the new normal in education, even in the online world we can reiterate to learners to observe the Netiquette in using their social media accounts as netizens in the digital age. Through this MATENAKAN CREED, the students will keep their values intact. It will also continuously produce a well-disciplined students that will be an asset in the community.

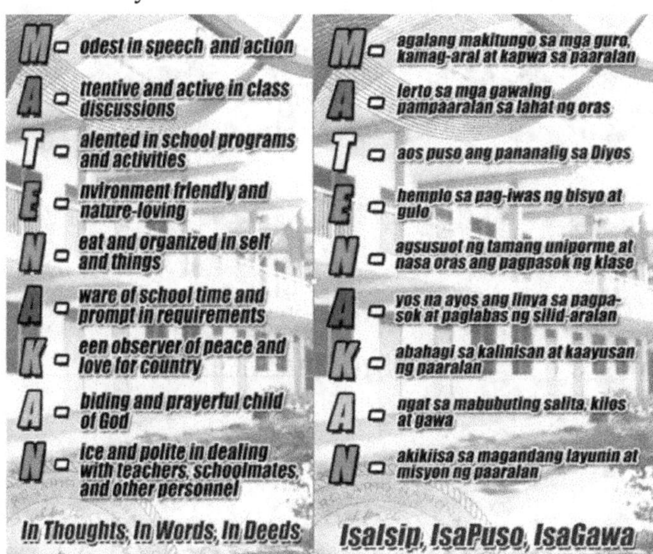

Great Unknown...

In The Eyes Of The Students

*The Greatest Reward of Teaching
is the
Priceless Appreciation of Students.
In the Eyes…*

Of the Students...

Of the Students...

In the Eyes...

Of the Students...

In the Eyes...

Of the Students...

Of the Students...

In the Eyes...

Of the Students...

In the Eyes...

-> NakikipagFambam o bonding
sa mga kasayahan namin!

Of the Students...

In the Eyes...

Of the Students...

Of the Students...

In the Eyes...

->Kahit anong sakit ng ulo ang ibigay namin sa kanya ay kinakayanan niya dahil mahal niya kami☺

Of the Students...

In the Eyes…

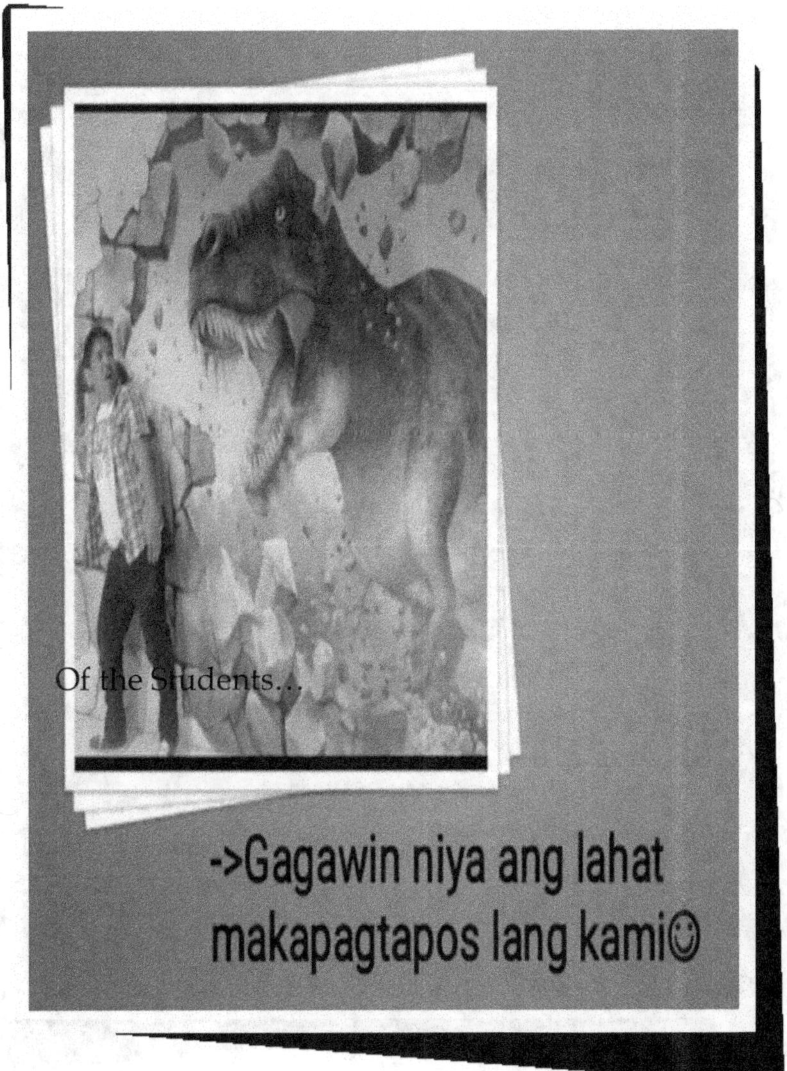

Of the Students…

In the Eyes…

In the eyes...

->Kahit anong sakit ng ulo ang ibigay namin sa kanya ay kinakayanan niya dahil mahal niya kami☺

Of the students...

In The Eyes...

Of the Students...

In the Eyes...

->Lahat ng pagsubok
ay kinakayanan niya

Of the Students...

In the Eyes...

Of the Students...

In the Eyes...

-> Inaayos ang mga gusot
at pagkakamali namin

Of the Students...

COLORLESS

RAINBOW

Unknownymously Yours

The SEQUEL

Colorless Rainbow...

Colorless Rainbow is the sequel of Test-imony and Mess-ages. This is a 2 –part life story. This 2nd part can only be thoroughly understood if one will read the 1st part which can be found in the Silver Lining book. Book 1 featured the gloomy childhood years. The broken years weren't only about struggles on poverty.

Unlike other stories, struggles were beyond rags situation. The violent thunder and deadly lightning in life made the man wait for the Silver Lining to appear. The man thought it took years when God finally smiled at him. After the raging storms, the colorless rainbow in his life is now a colorful sight to behold.

Unknownymously yours II...

Colorless Rainbow...

THE LAST COIN...
Though he knew from the very start
His parents had no means to support
his plan to pursue college
The risk taker went to a place
to apply for scholarship
with just one last coin

THE DEFORMED COLLEGE UNIFORM...
Coming from a public school
where deformed uniform
seems not a big deal
He didn't expect studying
in a semi-private college
He would receive discrimination
From a schoolmate for a deformed uniform

THE TYPEWRITER STORY...
He was taking his typing lesson
when he accidentally hit a button
that made the typewriter malfunction
This incident made him cry and pray all night
for he had no money to pay
once it won't function anymore.

Unknownymously yours II...

Colorless Rainbow...

RAINING INSIDE...
The rain inside actually seemed normal
His siblings and he used to experience
this almost every night
Every time his parents fight
The noise, the rain, the fight

THE BLOOD ...
A blood, there's a blood
Flowing from his mother's head
When a nail hit his mother's head
Due to his father unforgivable action
The day when his hatred over his father
became deeper

THE NPAs
Every time his parents fight
His siblings and his' custody was always the
subject
They experienced transferring
from time to time
from one house to another
They were the famous broken family

Unknownymously yours II...

Colorless Rainbow...

THE FEAR HE SAW...
The Fear he witnessed from his mother
Was the fear of a vulnerable battered wife
for the longest time
The first time he saw his mother
helpless and defenseless
He would want to kill his father.

WHEN THE LIGHT TOTALLY DIMMED...
Signs of nervous breakdown
were seen on his mother
His mother was talking alone
That incident pained him a lot
A smart boy he was
Couldn't do anything
For his sick mother

THE FURY...
He believed his mother's illness
All rooted from ill-mannered people
who misunderstood his mom.
That day, the fury
of a young man grew incessantly.

Unknownymously yours II...

Colorless Rainbow...

I LOVE YOU, GOODBYE...
March 19 when his sick mother passed away
He was just starting his career
to fulfil his promises to his mom.
That was the colorless rainbow happened
In his and siblings' lives.

.

ELECTRIC FAN...
When his father went home drunk
His father's brutal words made him
burst out his feelings to his father.
The eruption of emotions made him tell his father
"You should be the one died not my mother".
His father threw him the electric fan.
He threw it back to his father.

THE UNEXPECTED NEWS...
He was hospitalized
due to stomach ache
That night he was discharged,
his father was about to be
admitted in the same hospital.
He had no idea,
his father would pass away
That night was the last time,
He and his father saw each other.

To be continued on Book III
Unknownymously yours II...

Disclaimer: Image not mine / cttro

Life is a living book. Be sure it inspires.

REWRITE THE STARS

When God Smiled At Me

Rewrite the stars...

The man thought it took years when God finally smiled at him. Since he was a child he was patiently waiting to gaze the colorful rainbow. The trials he went through blocked his eyes. This only made him see colorless rainbow.

Many nights he tried to gaze stars but he only saw darkness. Because there were no nights that he didn't witness a battlefield. His growing up years were not ideal. He didn't grow up in an ideal environment. He witnessed how his parents fight. He witnessed how broke his family.

When God smiled at me...

Rewrite the stars...

No child would ever wish and dream to have a childhood years like his.

No one would also choose to have a broken family like his.

He was a product of broken family not once, not twice, actually he couldn't really remember how many times.

What he only remembered is a dark past. A violent past he wouldn't love to go back. While he was writing this book 2, he had to stop every now and then. Tears were rolling down on his face, his heart was beating fast and throat was blocked made him to hardly swallow as he went back to trying times of his life. He hated the life he had.

He thought God abandoned him. He felt God turned His back on him.. He stopped serving God. He started to rewrite his own stars. The stars he only wanted to see.

Worst storm came. His mother died who was his world then. Everything fell apart. He couldn't forgive himself. He deeply hated his father, too. Months passed, his father died too on the same year.

When God smiled at me...

Rewrite the stars…

He didn't know where to go. He was like an orphan. He had to move on with his life and support his siblings.
Pass forward…God of second chance showed him the way. He who had many realizations in life is now enjoying the rainbow God has promised him.
These realizations have taught him to share with others who are going through and facing the same storms of life.
Stormy seasons of life just come and go. Storms don't last forever. Storms make us strong and wise. They are life tests to pass and lessons to live.
. When life seems dark and cloudy, don't try to stop it. Let the storms fall. Storms help us to clear our paths. Not all storms present in our lives stop us to grow and bloom.
In the words of Vivian Greene (2006), Life isn't about waiting for the storm to pass; it's about learning to dance in the rain.
And as we all bravely sing, We can make it through the rain. There's always a rainbow after the rain.

When God smiled at me…

Rewrite the stars...

Stories are shared not to draw attention or reaction from the public. It is not about making himself (story-teller) a celebrity whose life is an open book. Its main purpose is to inspire people to keep going despite the storms that raging their lives. It is also to shed light on some issues that each had experienced or might be experiencing.

Sharing life story is sharing one's heart, one's soul, one's triumph and one's defeat through the years. It is not about making oneself famous from the sad story. Stories like these should not be a subject of criticism, mockery and discrimination. We have no idea how the story teller prepared himself mentally, emotionally and spiritually to let other people come into his untold stories by opening his private life.

When God smiled at me...

Rewrite the stars...

These stories are product of sad and happy experience, dark and light moments, weakness and strengths, falling and rising hurting and healing, pain and joy.

True to life stories mean they really exist in this world. Real people with real success stories on rags to riches, losing to winning, rejection to acceptance, dream to reality and stories of survival in this cruel world should serve as a reminder that God is in control whatever situation a person has. Rainbow stories become colorful testimonies of faith in doubt, hope in sufferings and love in rejection. They continue to move people.

This pandemic, self-help books are best served during these hard-hitting and trying times. The world has been lockdown for almost 6 months now as of this writing.

When God smiled at me...

Rewrite the stars...

People are waiting for ray of hope and beam of light that this, too, shall pass. No matter how one rewrites the stars of life, God will surely take in charge. When God smiles and rewrites the stars of life, everything will fall into place.

R - ainbow always comes after the rain. Patiently wait for it.
E – ncourage the disheartened. Be encourager in a world full of critics.
W – eaknesses are strengths in disguise. All have own shares of imperfections.
R – edeem and forgive yourself. Forgive others too to move on in life.
I – t's okay not to be okay. This, too, shall pass. God knows your pain.
T – rust God and His plans. Don't lean on your own understanding.
E – njoy each day with family and friends. Life is too short to waste it for nothing.

When God smiled at me... 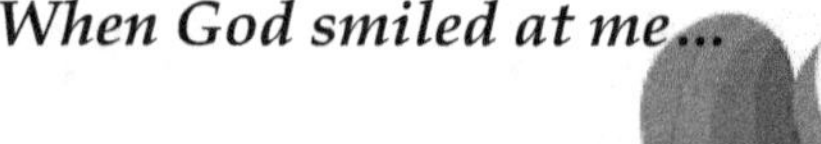

Rewrite the stars...

T – reat people with kindness. Each is facing a battle we don't know.
H – ope for better tomorrow. Be a source of hope too to hopeless.
E- mbrace life no matter what it offers. Live a life that inspires and touches.

S – ilver lining appears behind each cloud. Be a silver liner. Be a blessing
T – ake life lightly. Don't be too hard to yourself.
A – cknowledge God in all things. Everything we have comes from Him.
R – ise and Shine. Life is not over yet. We are all work in progress.
S – eek God first and make Him the center of your life. He is everything in life.

When God smiled at me...

Rainbow

Journal

A 40-Day Reflection Challenge

*Every gising
is a colorful
blessing.
Count your
Hues of
blessings.
Be Blessed & be
a Rainbow
Blessing.*

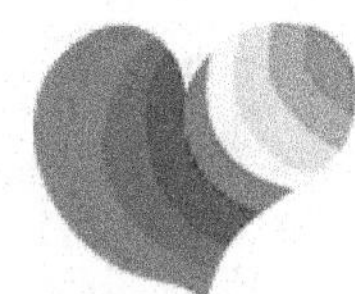

Day 11
Dear RB Journal,

____

____

____

Day12
Dear RB Journal,

____

____

____

Day13
Dear RB Journal,

____

____

____

Day 14
Dear RB Journal,

____

____

____

Day 15
Dear RB Journal,

____

____

____

____

Day 16
Dear RB Journal,

____

____

Day 17
Dear RB Journal,

____

____

Day 18
Dear RB Journal,

____

____

Day 19
Dear RB Journal,

____

____

Day 20
Dear RB Journal,

____

____

____

Day 21
Dear RB Journal,

____

____

____

Day 22
Dear RB Journal,

____

____

____

Day 23
Dear RB Journal,

____

____

____

Day 24
Dear RB Journal,

____

____

____

Day 25
Dear RB Journal,

____

____

____

____

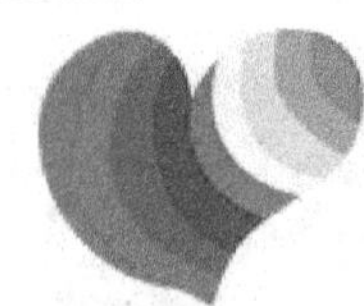

Day 26
Dear RB Journal,

____

____

____

Day 27
Dear RB Journal,

____

____

____

Day 28
Dear RB Journal,

____

____

____

Day 29
Dear RB Journal,

____

____

____

Day 30
Dear RB Journal,

____

____

____

____

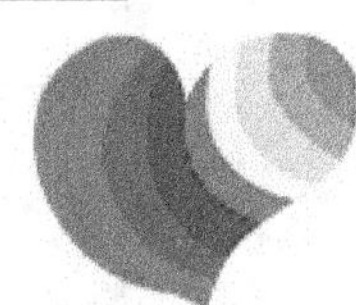

Day 31
Dear RB Journal,

____

____

____

Day 32
Dear RB Journal,

____

____

____

Day 33
Dear RB Journal,

____

____

____

Day 34
Dear RB Journal,

____

____

____

Day 35
Dear RB Journal,

____

____

____

____

Day 36
Dear RB Journal,

____

____

____

Day 37
Dear RB Journal,

____

____

____

Day 38
Dear RB Journal,

____

____

____

Day 39
Dear RB Journal,

____

____

____

Day 40
Dear RB Journal,

____

____

____

____

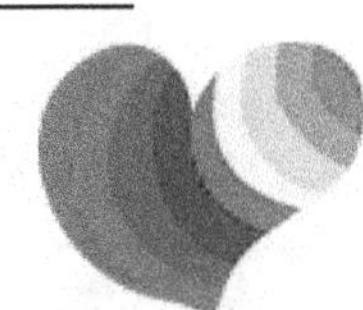

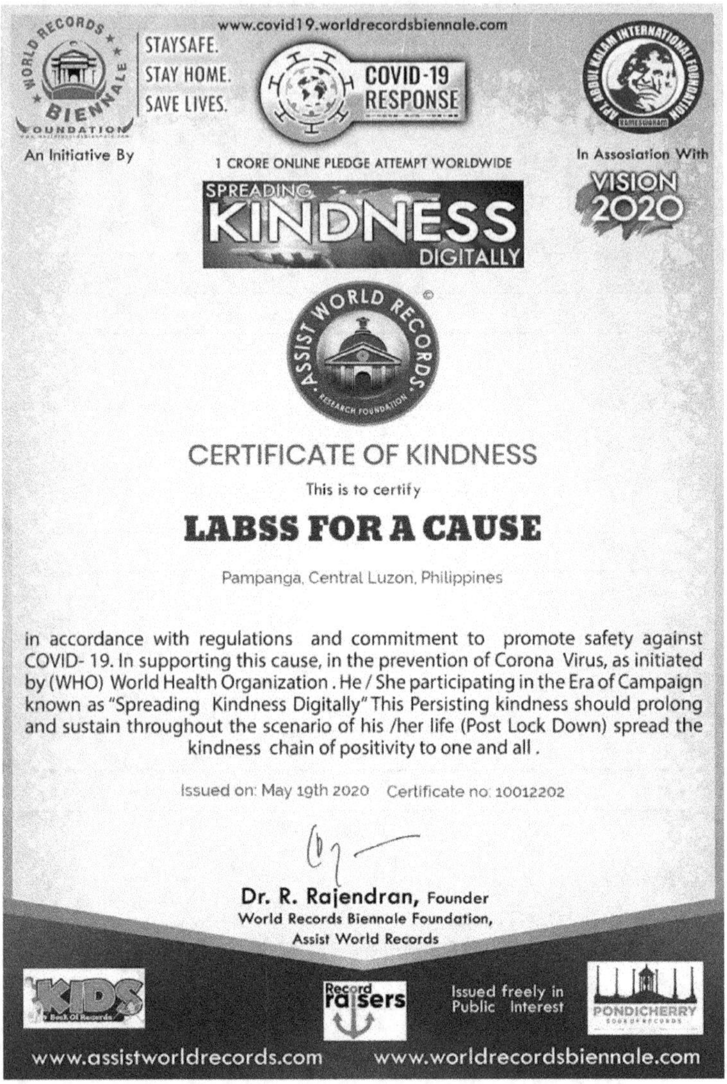

This pandemic…
Be a Rainbow of hope and light.
Spread Kindness, Positivity and
Good Vibes.

Dedication

I wholeheartedly dedicate
my book, RAINBOW
to all who have become a rainbow
in someone else's cloud.

To my family

My va-Leny-tine, Leny S. Ocampo
and two handsome and bright sons,
aweSam, Rabbi Samuel and
brightSky, Raziel Schuyler
who have been my inspirations in life

to my parents and siblings

my parents, Arnel and Imelda Ocampo
whom I dearly love despite their marital
indifference
and my siblings, Aimee, Arnold, Ace and AC
who, like me, braved the same storms in life.

Acknowledgement

Profound Thanks
to
My colleagues and friends namely;
Mesdames Weng, Teckles, Pines
Cathy, Rems, Carol and Cyrell
who have shared their WAGI Rainbow Stories.

Forever Grateful
to
God, who has blessed me
with rain3ow ye4rs.

Special Thanks
to
Marites C. Ritumalta
Builder of Dreams

About the Author

Mr. Angel Bryan Z. Ocampo is happily married to a fellow teacher, Leny S. Ocampo. He is a father of two namely, Rabbi Samuel and Raziel Schuyler.

He is a DepEd Teacher. He is a 2- time Division Gawad Parangal awardee as a Brigada Eskwela Coordinator.

He is the author of Silver Lining of Poetry Planet Publishing: Builder of Dreams.

More than being an author, he is an unknown cheerful giver behind the LABSS for a Cause family advocacy through his Seminar and Book.

After publishing Rainbow, his 2nd book, he is now writing his 3rd inspirational book and 1st book on education.

This Lockdown, nothing has stopped him, as he humbly received Mahatma Gandhi and Jose P. Rizal PEACE PRIZE awards from Institute for the Roma studies of Europe and Global Academy for Human Excellence respectively.

Published by Poetry Planet Publishing House
Edited and designed by Tess Ritumalta
Cover picture artwork credit – Anna Crystal Z. Ocampo
The author would like to acknowledge all the makers of different images used with disclaimer note of no copyright infringement intended/ not mine by the author/ credit to the rightful owner (cttro) . Images may contain their own copyright

www.ingramcontent.com/pod-product-compliance
Lightning Source LLC
Chambersburg PA
CBHW071947150726
47999CB00001B/347